The Bold News of Birdcalls

3/31/2021

For Michael
with best regards
to you in your
life and work,

Ed Morin

The Bold News of Birdcalls

Poems by

Edward Morin

Cover design by Shay Culligan
Cover photograph by Rogean James Caleffi on Unsplash

ISBN: 978-1-952326-70-7

Kelsay Books
502 South 1040 East, A-119
American Fork, Utah, 84003

For Camille, my best listener and reader

Acknowledgments

Poems in this collection, some of them in a different form, have appeared in the following publications:

Before There Is Nowhere to Stand: Palestine/Israel: Poets Respond to the Struggle, ed. Joan Dobbie and Grace Beeler (Sandpoint, ID: Lost Horse Press, 2012): "Fr. Holtschneider Considers Dr. Norman Finkelstein's Tenure"

The California Quarterly: "Hail Poetry"

Connotation Press: An Online Artifact: "Testament"

Cruel Garters: "During the Long War"

di-vêrsé-city Anthology: Austin International Poetry Festival (Austin, TX: Austin Poets International, 2017 and 2020): "The Academy" and "Juncos' Reunion"

Heartlands: "Inauguration, 2005"

The MacGuffin: "Buzz Cut" and "Icicles"

MidAmerica: The Yearbook of the Society for the Study of Midwestern Literature: "Yes" and "Aerial Combat"

New Letters: "Valentine's Day, 1972"

Out of Line: "Invisible Hand"

Peninsula Poets: "Bank Swallows," "Beneath the Bridge," "Epithalamion," "Housing for Wrens," "Marian," "Old School Ties," and "Song"

Ploughshares: "The Poem as a Deconstructed Car"

Poetry Leaves: "Best Friend"

Third Wednesday: "A Bird Story," "Depression," "Elegy," "Ladder Crash," and "Poetry Man"

Wetting Our Lines Together: An Anthology of Recent North American Fishing Poems, ed. Allen Hoey with Cynthia Hoey & Daniel J. Moriarty (Syracuse, N.Y.: Tamarack Editions, 1982): "The Big One"

Writers Reading at Sweetwaters: An Anthology of Poetry and Prose, ed. Chris Lord and Esther Hurwitz (Ann Arbor, MI: Word'n Woman Press, 2007): "Blue Jays"

"Elegy" won the *Third Wednesday* magazine's annual Poetry Contest Prize (2009); "Yes" won the Society for the Study of Midwestern Literature's Gwendolyn Brooks Poetry Prize in 2009, and "Aerial Combat" won it in 2019.

Eighteen of the forty-three poems in this book were published in the author's chapbook, *Housing for Wrens* (Somerville, MA: Červená Barva Press, 2016).

Contents

III. Endurance of Robins

IV. Passage of Swans

I. Noise of Blue Jays

Blue Jays

call "Thief! Thief!" I must
rise early. A nest of them
makes my street a proving ground
for mischief—flower pots
tipped over, barbecues raided,
sleep spoiled. They cruise by
carefree as sharks.

Last year robins lived here—
well mannered, industrious,
respectful of property.
One street over, cardinals
serenade. Their brownish young
are voluble, elaborate
with the modesty of talented
beginners.

Jays are from the underworld,
sinister as Dutch elm disease.
In high branches, once the dew
burns off, two exchange
piercing rubato screams
without a trace of warmth.

Then the whole pack bickers,
turning the neighborhood
into a tenement courtyard.
They won't leave in winter.
They'll stay—accusing each other
and the sparrows who make way
for them at feeding stations

until just one is left chattering
for himself against the world
and the bare oaks, crying:
This is home. This is home.

Buzz Cut

Mowgli wakes deprived of his world,
two-inch caramel-colored fur gone:
"Who am I in this stubbly skin?"
The vet is nowhere to be bitten.

What thin space for dignity
between this Persian hairlessness
and the first old exit from the womb.
Whiskers on a tiny head, filled

with eyes, jolt one breath at a time.
Before, the world floated. He tucks
his chin against short leggings. Housebound,
he mouths a dream of sweet spring birds.

Elegy

For Jim Goldwasser (1939-2000)

Between our afternoon and evening classes,
we ate cheap and talked shop at Maccabees
or McKenzie Hall. Two instructors fresh
out of grad school, we craved to write fine stories
and bring as many students as we could
by sleigh over the moonlit tundra where
Hemingway and Chekhov had left their tracks.

Walking to class, we would rehearse essentials:
"Have a good joke ready to break the ice,
and know beyond doubt that your fly is zipped."
When Phooey U. denied us tenure, you said:
"We bin thrun outta better joints dan dis!"
How clever you were to find steady teaching
in the same town for the next thirty years.

I became a nomad in jobs and friendships.
That time an aneurism almost killed you,
I panicked, worried your family with calls.
The main thing is to survive. And you did—
with a wife's care, baseball, and swimming pool.
You cultivated new friends into old ones
and gave your students reason to revere you.

Candid, humane, engaging raconteur,
who rarely strove to get work into print,
you saw the classroom as your medium
and taught compassion through love of the scrawl.
Your tadpoles grew into frogs who know what stories
sound genuine (and why), what gives us hope
in life and art, and is most likely to endure.

Valentine's Day, 1972

A bloody or a sudden end . . .
        —W.B. Yeats

As I opened for business winter mornings
the paint store on the strip mall felt
like an air-filled bottle floating on water.
Sweep, dust, put out stock—comfortable
routines after I had lost three jobs
and a tenure bid in just two years.
Nixon had ordered wage freezes to curb
inflation; bosses cheerily complied.
My part-time teaching paid child support.

Customers were scarce. Some had become
snowbirds and flown off to Florida.
A man in a suede jacket and fedora
strode in to look at contact paper.
We walked across the sales floor to racks
with smooth, vinyl-coated rolls for shelves
and flocked paper for cabinets and walls.
He looked prosperous, asked a few questions,
then thanked me and said he would be back.

At my desk in the back room I admired
some topaz earrings I planned to give the woman
I cared about when we would meet that night
for a dinner date at my apartment.
Chopin on the portable radio
seasoned the lunch I ate from a brown bag.
Locking the store, I left briefly to bank
the previous day's receipts. By three,
sun was shining through the plate glass windows.

19

The fedora returned. Trim, athletic,
he followed me to the contact paper.
"Stop there and keep your hands down,"
he said. My head and upper torso
screwed to the right: I saw a revolver
near my kidney. My hands reached for the sky
as in the movies. "Put your hands down!
Do what I say and you won't get hurt."
I knew I mustn't look at his face.

Stomach falling toward rubbery legs,
I walked ahead to the cash register,
opened it, emptied handfuls of money
into a paper bag, but dropped some coins.
"Leave the change on the floor," he said, marching me
to the back room, where I had to yield
reserves of small bills stashed in a paint can.
"Now where's the gun!" he rasped.
                              "There's no gun.
This isn't my store. You have to believe me."

My voice, bouncing back from the wall, scared me.
He said, "Put your hands behind you." I did.
My whole body weightless, eyes squinting,
I waited for the shot—and darkness.
An obstetrician haloed in light
said: "You have another baby girl."
I saw the beatified infant.
Next, my blond girlfriend appeared smiling,
back-lighted in a sheer long nightgown.

A scratching sound behind me. The robber
said, "I'm going to tape your hands together."
He wound my wrists solidly with duct tape,
then demanded, "Lay down on your stomach."
With ankles joined and chin slightly off
the floor, I could watch my radio
playing a Beethoven symphony.
Now that I couldn't possibly harm him,
my fear of the robber diminished.

His hands lifted the music, unplugged it.
I moaned, "Oh, no, not the radio!"
"Shut up," he snapped. "I oughta kill you—
you know you got it coming to you."
No syllable I could have uttered
would have helped me give him a right answer.
I saw myself in the Chicago warehouse
lying in my own blood with the gang
Capone massacred on Valentine's Day.

Final orders: "I'm going to walk out
the front door. When I'm gone, count to 200.
Don't get up until you finish counting.
His steps echoed, the front door bumped shut.
I counted, squirmed upright, hopped out to
the counter, and freed my feet with scissors.
My next customer was so surprised
to see my taped wrists she nearly dropped
the squirming toddler she was holding.

Knowing we were all intact, I marveled
at the thief's timing, efficiency,
and clearly stated goals and commands.
We had both worked synergistically—
he for money and I to survive.
The nickel and quarter on the floor
I threw into the cash register—
my way to refuse the bastard's tip.
Plainclothes police came and left. I rushed home.

Cora liked and wore the earrings I gave her.
Toasting with red wine before beef stew,
improved on its second day, we feasted.
Her forehead, limpid eyes, and smooth hair
scintillating in the candle light,
she listened to my energized tale.
Strong desire made me impatient
to reach the end. Finally she said,
"Leave your head and get into your body."

Gamblers are the most volatile lovers—
pouting children when they lose, titans
when luck goes their way. I hate gaming,
but today I'd won the biggest stake
imaginable—my own life.
In that little room, we celebrated
like citizens who parade, throw confetti,
sing in the streets. The war is over!
All the troops are   coming   home   now.

Bright moments make the worst bearable,
imbedded in memory as this dream is:
Pedaling a bike on a major street,
I slow with the traffic for a stoplight.
Suddenly I'm way up in the air.
Below, my wheels approach a stopped truck;
I squeeze the handbrakes and cease all motion.
For balance my foot must touch the street
but can't. I wake up, glad to be here.

Next day at the paint store, the other
managers phoned for particulars.
Customers looked like would-be robbers.
So I quit. My landlord, who did time
for manslaughter, told me: "You did right.
That crook told green kids you were a pushover,
and one of them would have popped you off."
They have to let you win once in a while
so you'll keep playing. It was only a job.

Icicles

Stilettos of ice,
as many as stabbed Caesar,
lengthening from the overhang
outside my back door. You shiny
stalactites in the cave of winter,
inversions of hope and every hint of good.
The snow that droops the snowdrift crab tree
mimics spring blossoms. The tree's last
orange fruit was eaten long ago by starlings.

February is a sallow miser who hoards
what little daylight is left in the world.
I could slip and break my bones on the doorstep.
But I wade out to the woodpile,
wrestle the crust off maple logs,
and haul them up porch stairs into the house.
With popcorn bowl, I'll face the roaring hearth,
roll red wine in a glass, and sing a song
to the thaw that will harvest every last one
of you gruesome drip-nose icicles.

Bank Swallows

are black-winged acrobats
flitting over sage and juniper:
their white throats fill with gnats and flies
they catch all day above
the bright hot dunes of Lake Huron.

While siskins hide in cool pines
and preening kingbirds avoid the hunt,
two of these magnificent tricksters
squeak, flank, and sally like bats raiding
the beach where we swimmers lie like fossils.

They take turns plunging scissor-tailed,
"now you see me—now you don't," in under
the crest of a sand cliff, staying buried
just long enough to feed the young
without breathing much air inside,
then catapult out into blue sky.

Remember, love, our barefooted climb
in dry roots thin as hair, up the sliding,
steep sand hill? The nest's double doors
are two holes shaped like half-closed eyes,
too small to get a hand through.

The mates flutter and scold above us,
flashing sharp wings in the burning sun,
throwing shadows the size of hawks.
Our talk is being heard in somebody
else's home. Everybody is scared.

Invisible Hand

Theater empty. Lines from an old part
come to me: a walk-on cameo—
grey-suited—fedora askew—
made up extra dark around the eyes.

Tonight, I'll be the one who finds
families having an argument,
the working poor running in place,
drivers sleeping on their car keys.

By the end of the second act
I'll have separated those people
from all their earthly goods.
Nothing left for them but the street.

I'll relax secure in my role,
toss off a free drink afterwards.
The stage crew hammers. No scripts in sight.
No one understands the title of the piece.

My worn hat on a nail, deep-
pocketed, freshly-pressed suit ready
for me to slide into, I don't know
why I kick the dressing room trash can.

Where are the losers whom I must
confront? The director's bald head
splits the curtain, whispers: *Remember
to project an air of righteousness.*

Poetry Man

For Lawrence Pike (1932-1995)

Starting from Saginaw
at age sixteen, a hitchhiker
expecting to find work picking cherries
on Grand Traverse peninsula,
you found your stride taking chances—
mishaps by the bucketful and yarns
spit out like cherry pits in laughter.

I see your head bob in rhythm
to a thunderstorm rumbling outside.
Lightning flashes in your eyeglasses
as you sit cross-legged reading poems
aloud. You said your dreams always played
in monochrome; fed into your writing,
they were like classic films colorized
with a rainbow of your feelings
shown in quirky, corroded Detroit.

At ease walking on broken glass
in Highland Park or camping
at the bottom of the Grand Canyon,
you brought vistas to your dayhop students
and sent them off to discover their own.
They'd ask you: *How do I make my words sound*
authentic in my own voice? And you'd say:
Read the books in your hands—not just the crib notes.
Likewise, your voice became one of a kind.

Gut hanging over bell bottoms
or swim trunks, you waded through
your own and others' family griefs,
stretching your arms upward, grinning
like Ho Tai the carefree Buddha.

What fun I had barnstorming with you,
performing from Pontiac to Chicago,
and you were a hard act to follow.
When campus gigs became scarce for us,
we squeezed our poems edgewise through open
mics at local bars and coffee houses.
Seasoned hams like us love to hang out.

The stormy wit of your first book
calmed a little after you found Trudi.
When cancer dragged her from you,
you became Orpheus wandering
into Hades, returning each time
with a song more sensual than the last
until cancer, like the wave that had taken
your lover, finally swept you under.

Your sons and your friend Dawn eased your exit.
Forsythia draped yellow cascades
over cold-closed purple crocuses.
Without you, our scribblers group argued
like kids over who's on, who's off the marquee
of recognition. We got tired of
raking through one another's manuscripts.

In isolation I ask myself:
Why go on writing? Is it for glory?
promotion? a fee? self-help? or even
to knock another poet out of the ring?
Larry, I celebrate and share your
compulsion: fire smoldering in the belly,
rising to enchant the heart and brain
and fly out of the mouth, as a gift.

Testament

The patriarchal tale of Eden
strikes many post-modern eyes as flawed.
As go-between for the Snake, Eve lures
naïve Adam to taste the orange of ruin
and takes most of the rap for Man's Fall.

Rather, from the beginning a reptile
resides as part of each human brain,
telling us to please only ourselves.
It shuns debates over tasks, waiting,
doing homework, playing well with others.

We rarely sense the snake in others
at checkout counters, in office buildings,
on soccer fields. To well-behaved folks
a whispered "Hell is other people!"
becomes a roar in bars and casinos.

Suppose I scorn convention, think myself
a marvel, write poems for weddings
and free drinks, lie drunk in the gutter,
kissed by Luna's tender rays—my one care
to find the most schnapps for the least coin.

Reckless self-indulgence gives command
to the reptilian brain in me
and all who fall: addicted gamblers,
big bankers strong-arming governments,
the recruit who kills as he is told.

Depression

Out back by the garage, the pumpkin tilts
where I set it on the barbecue grill.
Undeterred by gauzy mold in its head,
squirrels chewed a larger smile onto the mouth.
They'd finished off the seeds by Halloween.
The nose too is cratered, and teeth marks
show at the sides of the eyes like crow's-feet.

The years will ravage us like that:
lights gone, we'll wait for garbage day.
There is no comfort in imagining
eyebrows as originally carved.
Many of us have fought long to avoid
getting laid off. The moon reminds me now
through clattering oak leaves that I am losing.

Under its webbed arcade of mist
the world has finally run out of work.
Shadows like brunette hair growing
on a corpse cover the moon's caved,
jack-o'-lantern skull. The limp mouth
twists crookedly as during a stroke.
Loneliness is a feeling time has run out.

Yes

When Joe Sartori shook my left hand,
his grip locked in like a rock crusher.
"Not so hard!" his wife cried, "you'll hurt him."
I squeezed back with almost equal force
for a piss-and-vinegar moment
as, with a smile, he growled, "Yes, Yes!"

Home from college for the holidays,
I visited these middle-aged neighbors
at my mother's bidding, and for fun.
Biscotti and red vermouth appeared.
Joe smacked his lips, his polished face glowed,
and his baritone resounded, "Yesss!"

Martha talked enough for both of them.
Except for his left upper body,
Joe was paralyzed. From a wheelchair
he interposed his one syllable
with droll inflections, or shook his head.
His wife assured me, "He understands you."

She asked parentally about school.
As I described my courses, she said,
"How can your head hold all that knowledge!"
I hadn't told how much I forgot.
She thought our brains worked like pots. Joe's leaked.
I sensed he must have envied me mine.

I used to hear them argue next door,
she ranting at the end of her rope,
he yammering unintelligibly.
Pentecostals passing by their house
might have thought they heard Joe speak in tongues.
He was Catholic, as far as we knew.

When I was broke or girlfriends dumped me
and I feared the horrors of life's end,
Joe's predicament stormed into mind.
Fate gave him one word to last his life.
Not a bad choice, I still say out loud
to the night sky in witless affirmation.
Yes. Yes. Yes.

II. Melody of Wrens

Housing for Wrens

In April when forsythia explodes
overnight in yellow fireworks
like fresh popcorn along arcing branches,

and the goldfinch abandons olive drab
plumage to emulate forsythias' hue,
his stark ebony cap and wings a hat trick,

along comes the plain-brown-wrappered wren,
focused as a meter reader, from yard
to yard appraising birdhouses for nesting.

He darts between a brush pile and a gourd
I hung beyond reach in a redbud tree—
in and out a door hole the width of my thumb.

This friend of gardeners is a connoisseur
of bugs, his warbling song lasts into summer,
and lots of people want him for a neighbor.

Voice vibrations pulsate from chin through tall throat
and halfway down the chest. Such breath control!
What long, loud peals for such a little bell.

He shows off for peers when he calls a mate
or announces his territory, saying
to other wrens in earshot: "Stay away."

Once he finds a few properties, the female
arrives, the pair will tour them, and the one
she likes best is where they'll make their nest.

Being landlord to wrens requires
going along with the jenny. She churrs
insistently for a house that's clean.

I've scrubbed out detritus left from last year's
brood to make home pleasant for the new family.
No soggy mush on the floor will breed bird lice.

A small door well above the nesting cushion
keeps blue jays out. Cats kill, and scolding wrens
bray up a din to drive away those hazards.

If wrens choose to nest in my yard this year,
I'll keep my cats indoors, watch parent wrens
fly day-long insect brigades home, and hear

the feathered divo on a blossoming branch
belt out an energetic ode to joy
a quarter mile into the neighborhood.

Milk Train

Coursing by whistle stops in the wee hours,
the milk train gave passengers a slow ride while
hauling dairy freight between farms and towns.

One night in my fourth summer
I saw myself through the window glass
of a Milwaukee Road passenger coach
in Union Station. From the platform
my suddenly shortened parents waved,
then slid away in a smiling game
of now-you-see-me-now-you-don't.

Light strings and crossing bells whizzed past.
Fat Uncle Mike and his bride Mary
treated me as their own.
We celebrated with songs, crayons,
story books, and cat's cradle.
Someone in black uniform and visored cap
waltzed down the aisle punching tickets.
I laughed over a salty hard-boiled egg.

Next morning no ma or dad. Mary said,
"They're in Chicago." Whatever that was,
I couldn't have any just now.
What use were station stops
whose names the visor-man
clucked out like a cuckoo?

	Green Bay
Cows in the corn	
	Stiles Junction
Gaping box cars	
	Coleman
Potato fields	
	Crivitz!

37

Empty coaches

       Wausaukee

in switch yards

       Pembine

Cliffs dark red

       Iron Mountain next!

Long shadows
leaping from woods

       Channing, Michigan

Scary birch trunks
in mist

       Sagola

Finally the promised

       Crystal Falls!

All three of us fell
out of the train onto gravel.
I wailed and kicked
into the arms of two strangers
called grandma and grandpa,
who smelled wrong
and spoke an unintelligible tongue.

Is the Upper Peninsula important?
Of course. It has been the farthest end
of my life. My oldest memory.

A Bird Story

As boys with slingshots in the U. P.,
my pals and I roamed the woods shooting
rocks at small things that moved. After missing
scores of chipmunks and swallows, they wanted
shotguns to bag ducks and grouse. I killed
a cedar waxwing, then swore off hunting.

Back home with a pocket-sized bird book
my mother gave me for my tenth birthday,
I stalked tired migrants perched along their
flyway in miles-long Burnham Park
on Chicago's Lake Michigan edge.
From a safe distance in a corridor

of trees and shrubs, I spied a wood thrush
sitting guard duty on eggs. Today
so much forest habitat has been lost
that parasitic cowbirds invade nests
and drive down populations. I feel privileged
to have watched a thrush nesting in Chicago.

I can more easily recall birds' names
than those of some human acquaintances;
just one name suits a whole feathered species
that reliably shows up every Spring.
In a mixed flock, how subtly distinct
the white-throated and white-crowned sparrows are.

Keeping a "life list" interests me no more
than collecting stamps or antique bottles.
Eyes, the most spiritual of the senses,
dazzle the soul with cherished sightings,
as when indigo buntings fly through sunlight,
magically changing from black to bright blue.

Sometimes the canopy of deep woods rings
with one distant thrush's haunting descant:
Hello. You can't see me. Here I am.
This recluse trills its two voice boxes
like Pan's double flute, lifting the soul
until no aspiration seems beyond me.

The Academy

For Noam Chomsky

We three half-pints played on the back porch
of the second floor flat where I lived.
Dudley and I yearned to start school.
His younger brother Bobby asked us,
"What's a human bean?" And Dudley said,
"My dad knows about it. It's not
a bean you eat because it's people."

"With eyes and mouth and ears!" I shouted.
"Yep," said Dudley, "They're a kind of green."
"And do they walk around on their tips?"
I asked, "or have little feet extra?"
"They have feet," Bobby said, "and wear shoes."

We traipsed across the porch on tip-toes,
hands to our sides. Dudley and Bobby's
father was expert in so many things—
horseshoes, magic tricks, barbecues—
that I was eager to believe what
my two best friends said he told them.

Below us a red streetcar clattered
to a stop. Serious grown-ups emerged,
some of them shaded green through tree leaves.
Dudley counted: "One, two, three, four."
We watched them march in file to the curb
and said together: "Human beans!"

Since that first brush with metaphysics,
I've known innumerable bean counters
focused on dollars and the bottom line.
Our game was much happier than theirs.

Old School Ties

I think about you, Brad, classmate who aced
courses, seeming hardly to crack a book.
In track you were a sprinter of distinction,
while I struggled in middle distances.
We were hellions as a debating team:
I left-jabbed opponents with facts, you clinched
main points like a right cross bending the jaw.

We double dated to the senior prom—
jitterbugs fox-trotting "Stardust" at midnight.
I was catbird in the back seat of your
cerulean Mercury. My dream girl
in pastel opened like an orchid blooming.
Later when I lost her, your patient ear
heard my grief pour like beer foam from a pitcher.

You took on med school, starred in orthopedics,
finished in Palm Springs, and turned to writing.
I looked you up, learned you had won first prize
from Harry's Bar and American Grill
for parodying Hemingway's narration.
But you'd died. No chance to catch your deep-gut laugh
or even once see *you* cry in your beer.

Bolts in the Blue

1

My dad poured tangled nails into a jar,
assorted nuts and bolts into another,
and—into a third—hydra-headed screws
that love to pierce and hold resistant wood.
Lids fastened under a high pantry shelf
held the jars whose bright silver and brass shone
in beams of sunlight through a narrow window.
.

Like sweets kept out of small kids' reach, the contents
sometimes came down into my eager hands
when our fabricator built or fixed things.
In those days of toy trains, erector sets,
and Tinker Toys, I thought for quite a while
that the world could be rebuilt and improved
with the likes of fasteners from those jars.

My friends' dads and mine worked in factories.
He showed me how to fit a matching bolt
and nut, reciting the mantra: "Don't force it."
Taught by hardware's discrete edges, he said:
"There are lots of ways to do a thing wrong,
but there's only one way to do it right."
He kept our few possessions in good order.

2

Today junk clogs my basement, e-mail in-box,
and attic. The corners of my study groan
under stacks of stuffed manila folders,
dead relatives' pictures, prospectuses,
unread journals. Once a week, my hands dip
into the dry stream of shredded paper,
bagged and hauled to the curb for recycling.

The odd screws, nuts, and bolts I've been saving
won't fix new machines' modular, closed units,
which simply get replaced, once they're broken.
It's hard to know who made what anymore.
Proud Americans keep trying to force
our nut onto some other country's bolt.
How long and how many ways must we
keep trying to make mismatched pieces fit?

Glass jars refrigerate leftovers well;
my drawer for lids is so full it won't close.
If I'm out walking anywhere and see
a loose nut or bolt shining in the street,
I pick it up, bring it home, and drop it
into its dedicated jar. Perhaps
I'll find some undiscovered use for it.

Mighty Phragmites

1

The Great Black Swamp, once a hunting ground
of ten Native American tribes,
frightened settlers. After Mad Anthony
Wayne's Battle of Fallen Timbers,
they slowly filled in swampland for farms.
Except in the Erie Marsh, where clubs
of anglers and duck hunters dug channels
for their boats to capture "nature's bounty."

Carp play in shallow water there now.
The robust, invasive super reed,
Phragmites australis, rules the wetland.
This tough brown grass, the giraffe of reeds,
wags tasseled seed heads in any wind.
Dense rhizomes throw off gallic acid,
which ultra-violet light turns mesoxalic—
toxins that vanquish even other reeds.

For decades wastewater treatment plants
used phragmites to filter pollutants.
This genotype of the common reed
slurped them up, thrived, and migrated westward
from Atlantic shores through low lying
Ohio, Michigan, Indiana—
the drained, old Black Swamp, past Illinois
up to lakeside shallows of Green Bay.

2

In morning mist, the spectral, dingy
phragmites invades expressway ditches;
roots like octopi tangle downward
in waist-high water, and they climb wet slopes
away from their base in disturbed swamps.
The reed's horizontal runners spread
sixteen feet per year, killing cattails
that might have harbored willows and poplars.

Gone are nesting yellowthroats. Water fowl
can't feed. Self-respecting muskrats won't dig
a den among those impacted roots.
This vegetative conquistador
makes open spaces impassable,
monotonizing roadways everywhere.
Maybe people have so many troubles
they can't afford to notice this one.

Why won't someone harvest it for profit?
break those suckers down for ethanol?
hire employees who'll burn it as gas?
make reeds for the world's bassoon players!
I'm told that in Europe grazing cattle
suppress the growth of the common reed.
Let's bring back herds of buffalo to munch
away these stands of ugly phragmites.

Beneath the Bridge

Variations on the Slovakian Folk Song "A Pod Mostom"

Beneath the bridge, beneath the bridge,
fish are swimming.
Beneath the bridge, beneath the bridge,
fish are swimming.
Pa has caught the finest one,
Ma will fry it crisp and done,
then we'll all dine.

Kiss me darling, kiss me darling
for I love you.
Kiss me darling, kiss me darling
for I love you.
Roses blossom in the spring
promising us everything.
Wishes ripen.

Where are the fish? Where are the fish?
Gone or eaten.
Where are the fish? Where are the fish?
Gone or eaten.
Same for us in grief and strife.
Leaf mold seasons every life
as the sun shines.

The Big One

Some days you eat the fish,
some days the fish eats you.

1

As with the picture puzzle of an angler
wading in a mountain lake, which I pieced
together when I was eight, wondering
what lurked beneath the broken surface, I say
after thirty-five years that with a fish
we never get the right point of view—his.

Maybe that's what fishing is about—trying
to see what goes on down there—little ones
devoured by bigger ones until the one Biggest
eats the next biggest and so ends the chain.
Would one of us do well to catch the Biggest
before it eats up all the other fish?

The share of bass, perch, trout, and pike I've caught
impressed me once, but it no longer does.
Last year off the coast of Mexico, I
caught a barracuda big as my arm,
but an inboard motor and two guides helping
are hardly what you'd call "do-it-yourself."

2

In a canoe on pine-rimmed Crooked Lake,
Leonard, who is eight, asks me, "Are there fish
in here that bite?" "Bite us," he means. I say:
"They could bite us, but they leave us alone
unless we grab them flopping in the boat
or on land. Some can bite small holes, which heal."
Five of us take two canoes in high sun
across deep water linked by weedy channels.
We troll with plugs and spoons, but no fish bite.
We swim and eat lunch on an island where
we catch sight of an eagle overhead.
He circles to watch us: this is his lake.

We start paddling the miles back in low sun;
this time the kids demand their own canoe.
Rachel, who dislikes fishing, takes the stern;
sports-minded Jocelyn in the bow wants racing;
Leonard sits low in the middle, trolling
a weedless silver spoon as they dash off.

3

Camille and I wait in a cove for bass.
Then in the channel weeds the pike start hitting.
With spoons, experience, and a landing net,
we easily catch four northern pike.
The soaring eagle, attacked by three kingbirds,
drops past the setting sun below the tree line.

Leonard's weedless spoon glides eventlessly
through every branch and channel till the last.
He says he has a snag and reels in
a speckled-looking log with starry teeth.
Consensus has it that his pike was not
much less than half the length of the canoe.

Seeing its fierce eyes and wide girth up close,
Leonard cries and lets out some line. He's played
with bluegills before now, but never dreamed
how scary a big fish's mouth can be.
All six hands hoist the pike up to the gunwale,
then it spits out the hook and plunges deep.

Envoi

That night over fish dinner, Leonard says,
"I don't fish for fun. I fish for food."
And somewhere in the slippery weeds, his pike
is growing bigger, waiting for the next
shiny morsel: aluminum canoe
or weedless spoon—or whatever shows up.

Idiot

Coaching a baseball team of twelve-year-olds,
I watched our second baseman take a bouncing
throw from the outfield as the runner
rounded third, brashly heading for home.
The buzzing nightlights made the ruddy
dust of the infield glow like a moonscape.

"Throw to the plate, Jason," I shouted.
But he ran the ball toward it instead.
"You idiot!" I called, "*throw* the ball."
After the base runner scored, Jason
handed me the ball and looked confused.
His parents rushed me—shouted a rhubarb:

"Apologize!" one snarled through clenched teeth.
"You called our son that word." It hit me:
Jason was slow witted. I'd forgotten.
The team's parents voted to bench me
for the next game. I apologized,
mourning Jason's plight along with mine.

Jason's mind was too good for that label.
I recalled how in the early grades
schoolmates taunted me with the name "moron,"
goading me to fight or try to get smart.
Now that I'd acted really dumb, the mantra
"You idiot!" choked deep in my throat.

Ladder Crash

The sun in February shrinks snow banks
along the driveway, and ice dams drip
from rain gutters. On wet, steamy asphalt
I ratchet the extension ladder
high between dormer eaves on either side
that keep the ladder from lurching sideways.
One foot over the other up the rungs,
with a hammer and star-drill chisel
I chip ice slabs off the clogged gutter.

They crack, fall, and splatter below me
as dusk begins to settle. The Tao says,
"Know when to stop and you will meet
with no danger." I haven't listened.
The ladder top slides down past the ice dam.
The bottom clatters away from the house,
pulls the rung from my grasp. I fall feet first,
bend my knees for recoil, meet the ground.
One ankle explodes, the other knee rips,
and a forearm slaps hard on the pavement.

Pain stabs my right foot. I roll and sit up.
The ladder lies intact, spanning debris.
Splinted and sedated by the kind
EMS crew, I tour Emergency,
believing I am a torpedo
propelled back and forth through body-scan
chambers. The talus bone in my ankle
was split like a piece of firewood.
The surgeon told me to keep my weight
off that foot in the cast for three months.

With six weeks gone, I have six more to wait
while the world greens outside my window.
How well will I be walking? in pain?
or with a limp? None of us knows yet.
I mull my folly and the last things,
admire the beauty of my one good foot,
even file my tax return early.

Lao Tzu says, "He who loves his body
more than dominion over the empire
can be entrusted with the empire."
Let mine be plants and grass in the yard,
having the health to cultivate them.
Smell the flowers. Listen to the birds.

III. Endurance of Robins

Aerial Combat

for Camille

A pair of robins built their third nest
of the summer in our climbing rosebush.
They'd abandoned one nest after a heavy
cowbird chick suffocated their offspring.
Squirrels ate the eggs in their second nest.

I watched these skilled masons weaving grass
into mud mortar for a deep-bowled fortress
sturdy enough to last beyond one season.
Pitched high among red roses on tough canes,
it was protected by a moat of thorns.

With tail erect, the incubating female
learned to tolerate us passing gardeners.
One afternoon a red-tailed hawk appeared
viewing the nest from a thick phone line.
Both robins screaked an alarm. One buzzed

over its head, one perched dangerously close.
Eying the chicks who filled the nest, the hawk
ignored the parents' frantic commotion.
The agonizing standoff lasted till
the two of us waved our arms and shouted.

The smug hawk arched its wings and flew away.
After the chicks had fledged, I saw the mother
perch exactly where the hawk had been. I spoke
softly about our recent scare, and she
listened thoughtfully to every word.

During the Long War

The shoes strewn on the floor discredit
everything about us, even drinking water.
The Moody Blues sing "Days of Future Passed."
Darling, we have been together four days

burning our bodies at both ends. We are
almost out of wine. The DJ is selling
popcorn on the night stand, and every
passing car hums an eviction notice.

Each toy is a dead toy, people, rocking
somewhere, thinking whatever it is you love
loves you. As our goods burn in the alley,
we watch like tree toads holding on with all

fours to a paper flower. A stale wind
blows the curtain. Our pillows turn into
large stones. We lie against them crying to
the sun, *Set quickly,* and to the dawn, *Be soon.*

The Poem as a Deconstructed Car

On a narrow street without a sign
in New Haven, outside the apartment
of the well-known critic, stands his royal
blue sports car with the key in the ignition.
The world knows his magnanimity
and he has never been unkind to me.
He won't mind my taking a little spin.
He must be napping and it's not right
to wake him. I drive with a near full tank
sloshing around corners, the larky wind
twittering my ears. Soon I must tool back
to recoup our parking space before it's gone.

It's gone. I scavenge over several blocks
but can't find even a pit stop anywhere.
He'll get quite angry with me when he wakes
and finds his auto absent from its place.
Fortunately, this is one of those new
deflatable kind. Unscrewing a valve,
I fold and square the vehicle neat
as a flag, then make ready my excuse.
Knock. Nobody comes. Snoring inside.
I chew on the pliant edge of a bumper.
Leaning the soft, flat-bundled waif against
the mighty door, I lope away on tiptoe.
You can't show any more respect than that.

Inauguration, 2005

What a bizarre security mania
commandeered the Avenue Pennsylvania:
stuffed shirts marched in a victory parade
to flaunt the grandeur Cash had made.
The First Lady wore her ermine coat,
while George leered in an all-day gloat,
and corralled leftists yelled, "yo' mama!"
Prime Time embraced this melodrama.

At the Capitol swear-in, all social classes
listened in tears and froze their asses.
The Inaugural Boy spoke loud and clear:
"Kumbaya and all that, we're for freedom, ya hear!"
He told the plebs an old enigma:
"Float SSA—being poor is no stigma."
After lobster and portabella mushrooma,
the band struck up "Halls of Montezuma."

By the end of the day George was feeling droopy,
yet to every ball Laura dragged her poopie.
She would have waltzed if they'd had the chance,
but her bozo doesn't drink *or* dance.
Once home, "W" cried, "Hey lookie,
Laura, we can have some nooky."
She groped him and hollered "Holy Osamas!
WMDs inside his pajamas."

Father Holtschneider Considers Dr. Norman Finkelstein's Tenure

1. *Furor Scholasticus*

We hired him as a hot property.
His trailer, laden with publications,
radiated prestige which DePaul needed.
Recommendations and teaching record
shone like finest Tiffany jewelry.
Who cared if Gotham universities
denied him tenure? We missed that omen.
After six years with us, he's published more,
counting translations into foreign languages,
than all the rest of my Liberal Arts faculty.
Lord save us, the mere mention of his name
makes plaster fall from my office ceiling.

He's a nice enough guy until he starts
talking about the Palestinians.
Then he becomes a bulldog who won't let go
of his bone. He told me he has been sharing
their miseries every summer in the West Bank.
I asked him why he sniffs out all that trouble.
He smiled and answered, "Because it's there."
Behind his growl I sensed compassion,
a strange hunger and thirst for justice.

Committees voted 9-3 and 6-0
to grant tenure; then an avalanche
of complaints accused administrators
and this son of holocaust survivors
of being anti-Semites. Embarrassment.

Norman's rival in Poli Sci asked
Harvard lawyer Alan Dershowitz
to find mistakes in Norman's publications.
He sent eighty pages called "faults and lies"—
none of it discredited Norman's work.
Alan's grudge was old news after Norman
exposed faked sources in Alan's book,
The Case for Israel, written by committee.
 On Amy Goodman's radio program
Democracy Now, Norman told Alan:
"You don't even know what's in your own book."

2. Governance

Give me a break. My job as President
is to make DePaul the best Catholic
University in America.
We're already the biggest. In my field,
Policy, good feelings and decorum
grease the chutes for donor contributions.
Samuel Johnson defined scholars as
"harmless drudges." They're the kind I like—
compulsives who just write history
and don't go rabble-rousing on the road.

By speaking in high profile venues,
Norman gave us bad public relations.
I'm "Mr. Outside" at this institution
and can't stand to see our image tarnished.
Dr. Johnson said of free speech: "A man
may express any opinion, and any other man
may knock him down for it." Alan's crew tried.

I kept the decision out of their hands.
We Vincentians put great store in "personalism":
only persons have souls, every one matters
and needs respect, including all our donors,
despite their intellectual limitations.
Vincentian Personalism would require
Norman to show respect even toward Alan.

He could have tried talking nicer to him
instead of launching his own Norman Conquest.
Why has controversy been the Catholic Church's
middle name? We need charity just to keep
from killing one another. Frankly,
our board, administrators, and core
faculty are corporate DePaul;
adjuncts, "tenure tracks," and grad assistants
just work here. I pray we all know our places.

3. Bon Voyage

Thank God we worked out a deal. For his office
and the year of classes to which he was entitled,
I gave what professionals expect:
praise and long, paid leave—a bronze parachute.
He may do well on speaking tours, but complains
that our actions blackball him and he'll never
teach again on an American campus.
He loves to teach and students love him,
especially those who sat in at my office
and went on a ten-day fast for his sake.
Some wiseacres called me Pontius Pilate.

I wish Norman well. His case is not unique.
The 16th-century Augustinian scholar,
Fray Luís de León, ran afoul of the Inquisition
for saying the Latin Vulgate was
a poor translation of the Hebrew Bible.
The son of Jewish conversos, he turned
The Song of Songs into the vernacular.
It got an "R" rating, so he spent five
horrible years in the pen. Returning to
Salamanca, he began his first lecture
with the words "As we were saying yesterday. . . ."

These days one doesn't find safe haven
such as Salamanca gave Fray Luís,
but Norman deserves a niche somewhere
in anyone's backyard except ours.

The Bernie Madoff Hustle

To a tune something like "Barney Google"

Bernie Madoff
made off with twenty billion cash.
Bernie Madoff
stole his clients' hard-earned stash.
He built a Ponzi scheme around his sons and brother.
If she were alive, he would have bilked his mother.
Bernie Madoff
made off with twenty billion cash.

Bernie's assets
made good news that got around.
Bernie's assets
kept going up but seldom down.
Investors believed their stocks and bonds were real,
but they were a fairy tale told by a heel.
Bernie's assets
became bad news that's still around.

Ruthie Madoff
hid ten million, then hid five—
Ruthie Madoff—
before the federals did arrive.
Police asked her, "Where did you put that money!"
She said, "That's my golden parachute, honey."
Ruthie Madoff
hid ten million, then hid five.

Ira Sorkin—
big time lawyer Bernie knows.
Ira Sorkin
pleaded his case until its close.

Victims blamed him for their wallets being leaner;
some thought he helped Bernie take 'em to the cleaner.
Ira Sorkin—
big time lawyer Bernie knows.

Sheryl Weinstein
was Hadassah's CFO;
Sheryl Weinstein
gave Bernie her Foundation's dough.
Her book explains it wasn't very nice
being the only victim Bernie screwed twice.
Sheryl Weinstein
was Hadassah's CFO.

Poor Mark Madoff
was his father's trusted aide,
Poor Mark Madoff
learned the truth and felt betrayed.
He couldn't bear the burden of his family name,
so he hanged himself under a cloud of shame.
Poor Mark Madoff
was his ol' man's sorry aide.

Bernie Madoff
once was everybody's friend.
Bernie Madoff
smiled until the bitter end.
People who thought Bernie had a great big heart
now want to throttle him and tear him apart.
Bernie Madoff
once was everybody's friend.

Best Friend

Crew-cut Archibald in the house next door
has Annie living with him for the summer.
Charming how they saunter to work each morning,
hand in hand swinging past the irises.

In the garage with her stored furniture,
Ann keeps a black spaniel. She walks him muzzled.
Archie says: "He'll bite anyone but Annie—
the best obedience college won't change him."

Ann patiently explains her pooch's merits,
how harsh treatment at the pound caused biting.
Tail wagging, leashed, he's moist-eyed on the lawn
and scans each passing leg for his main chance.

When I step out my back door after dark,
the locked-up dog growls like a junk car starting.
Goose bumps raise the hair on my arms. I talk
toward his prison wall to calm both of us:

"You're going to roast or freeze as temperatures
change in the garage. Build relationships
on only love or hate, and none will thrive.
Love me, love my dog? Don't count on it, mutt!"

Adjunct Winslow's Discourse

Teaching Introduction to Fiction
at a Harvard of the Midwest, I saw
ambitious students chafe at lecturing
and teach themselves instead, so I played
Socrates, asking leading questions.
Of two score enrollees, almost half
were pre-med or pre-law who wanted
a challenging, rewarding elective.

The day I returned their mid-term test,
some caviled about acceptable answers.
One smart, articulate brunette named
Eunice led the charge through Erdrich's
The Beet Queen and James Joyce's "The Dead."
She wore a tight T-shirt of one-inch
white-and-blueblack horizontal stripes
accentuating her endowment.
While explaining the servant Dorine's
hard life in Flaubert's "A Simple Heart,"
I wondered whether Eunice's cup size
was C, D, or oh-my-god! How much
of what was there was optical illusion?

After class she advanced to the front
with three classmates armed with test papers.
Formidably arguing her points,
Eunice embodied Aristotle's
definition of rhetoric: "the use
of all available means of persuasion."
I couldn't be fair to the fairest one
without slighting her ogling classmates.

No pillowy suasions for me. She had
the persona of a heavyweight
coming on toe to toe. I backed against
the chalkboard, held the chalk tray, and said:
"What are you trying to do—get into med school?"
No one spoke. She turned on her heels and left.

Hail Poetry!

*If customers think your fresh fish department is great,
there's a high probability they think your whole store
very good.*

—Greg Josefowicz, President*
Borders Group Inc.

The CEO of Borders says,
"We sell almost no poetry,
but we'll keep stocking it because—
like fresh fish in a grocery—
if people think your fish is good,
word spreads throughout the neighborhood."

Shelley's poems cruise like sailfish,
Frost's taste as salty as Maine cod.
Their blithe admirers feel unselfish
spending on cookbooks (they've found god).
Then they'll buy books on politics,
self-help, love, jobs, and money tricks.

New poets published by small presses
are hooked like flounder, hauled to port,
eyes fixed upon a mermaid's tresses.
Small numbers make their shelf life short:
quickly they're boxed and set outside,
the stench swept off by morning's tide.

---

*After several years as an executive of the Jewel-Osco supermarket chain, Mr. Josefowicz was at the helm of Borders booksellers from 1999 to 2006. He turned over its online operation to Amazon, Inc. about five years before Borders' bankruptcy.

Juncos' Reunion

for Gary Snyder

March fooled us by going out like a lion
and so far, April has played copycat.
Frost coats the grass. Some dark-eyed juncos
glean among husks beneath the bird feeder.
All are female: mouse gray heads and backs
have blended with winter earth while they flocked
in sisterhood separate from males,
who would scare them away from scarce food.

Suddenly two dark slate-backed males dive
to the ground and joust without pecking.
They flash brilliant white tail stripes, then bolt
away in a chase. The females keep feeding.
By now males have no wish to badger them.
Lucky for male juncos and the species
that in any season they contend
with individuals of only one sex.

Lilac and magnolia buds are bulging.
Juncos' tiny bills can't do much damage.
They don't sing much, but can they forage!
Amazing that females change their minds
so easily about those jocko bullies;
they seem the most forgiving of all females,
or else they just have short memories.
They wait demurely for the sound of feathers.

IV. Passage of Swans

India Dreams: An Ekphrastic Poem Based on a Composite Photograph

Faith is the bird that feels the light when the dawn
is still dark.

                  —Rabindranath Tagore

At Benares, renamed Varanasi,
holiest of India's seven sacred cities,
Hindus come to bathe in the Ganges River.
Some pray to die in this holy place,
freed from endless *karma,* joined with the One.

The white-haired man revealed in profile
against barren yellow sand wears all white—
a *dhoti* draping to his bare feet,
shirt-like *kurta,* a folded *chadder* shawl
on one shoulder. Mist rises over water.

Hands clasped, head bowed in contemplation,
the elder stands alone, except for a flock
of swans flying past in the blue-black sky.
An artist photographed him near a shrine
and culled the swans from a Mughal painting.

This pious man has lived through the stages
of celibate student and married householder.
The Veda recommends a third step:
to don a forest hermit's robe of poverty
and bring his wife with him, if she's willing.

They haven't talked much about this calling.
He fears he couldn't handle it by himself.
Like a bird with a string tied to its foot,
his mind flies every-which-way till exhausted,
then alights back to the place it's moored.

Will swans carry his imperishable soul
for transmigration to a newborn body?
When he has to become incorporeal,
losing memory of his former self
seems worse than falling into a crevasse.

As a child of the West, preoccupied
with our "gods of the screen," I feel refreshed
seeing him concerned with his soul's estate.
We all have to believe in something.
I believe he has ordered his life well.

Nina Hauser, "India Dreams, No. 1"
composite photograph on archival paper: "10 x 7"

Phases

from the Man in the Moon

Embarrassment? A half-moon realizes
that losing face is only temporary.

Viewing my full face, the world finds time to
plant crops, dally, celebrate, reminisce.

In third quarter, I rise while people sleep;
the restless worry and prioritize.

The side you've never seen is glowing now.
Hop a shuttle if you dare. Look around!

Epithalamion

for Todd and Kelly Heisler

Now that tulips, irises, and lilies
are past, hot salvias and black-eyed Susans
herald the brightest highlight of the summer.
Todd and Kelly, having been together
much of the last millennium, finally said:
"This love of ours endures, so let's get married."

Awake, you lovers, to the cardinal's chirp
and starling's squeal. Let bridesmaids help the bride
adorn herself in stunning, tasteful raiment.
Today, Todd, put your camera aside.
Let other hands snap memorable pictures
of you, Love's subjects, radiant in the sun.

Here on Chicago's fabled Near North Side,
nymphs and satyrs finish a Gay Pride march.
Playing guitar, lyre, and tambourine
alongside our passing cars, they feint
jocose offers to join our procession
and ask respect for their own marriages.

The church door opens wide and lovely Kelly
comes down the aisle in step to joyful music.
The dapper, nervous bridegroom takes her arm,
welcomed by fragrant garlands and the smiles
of relatives who light candles showing
unity as the spouses pledge their vows.

Receiving line, champagne, and wedding cake
give every guest a chance to wish you well.
You newly-weds have learned each other's ways.
You'll take your chance at juggling in that three-ringed
circus—work, school, family—and yet stay mindful
of who you are and where you want to go.

Once the bouquet is tossed, the garter gone,
time may pass like music in a slow dance.
The happiness we wait for comes in moments,
sometimes by surprise, like a cherished photo
in a long roll of film, where turn of head,
the light, and feelings blend—as they do now.

Faith in each other and a generous spirit
will bring good luck and laughter to your door.
Perhaps you will have children who, like mine,
keep parents young in play and busy caring.
Leave hobgoblins of worry in the dust.
Look forward to the life you choose together.

Moments Musicaux

In memory of my sister Audrey (1937-2010)

1

I don't know what I'm scowling about
in that picture of me in short pants
at age three, sitting in grandpa's lap
on their front porch steps. My first answer
usually has been that I resented
Mother's leaving me so long a time
while she carried my sister to term.

And there she is just two steps down
swaddled in a blanket, held by Grandma.
Ma must be the one behind the camera.
Relatives congratulated me
for having a new baby sister,
Maybe I saw her as one more to blame
for my baffling abandonment.

Holding a ukulele with one hand,
I look ready to wring its stringed neck.
To this day I hate that instrument
and have never cared to take up another.
Instead, songs run through my memory
or past my lips as readily as breath.
I know that I will keep on singing,

2

In Chicago at Orleans Apartments
on Oakenwald, my bantam-weight sister
beat scarlet fever, humming herself
to sleep—*mi* to *do,* over and over.
In her early grades I walked her to school.
I still recall full names of little friends
drawn to her sunny disposition.

Our mother, a homeopathic nurse,
dispensed free health care to the neighbors
and shielded us from our old man's rage.
Before we knew the days of the week
we learned to hide from Dad's weekend binges.
Remorse would set in: he'd make us black cows
And sing the jingle, *Dad's Old-Fashioned Root Beer.*

He played horseshoes in the lot next door
and walked us to the Lake to catch perch.
Audrey sang with us in St. Ambrose choir,
led by our friend—waggish, blind Jim Wright.
She took piano lessons and got braces.
After the family moved to Roseland,
she turned into a striking beauty.

3

Frank was Irish with black, wavy hair,
quite a good dancer with a smooth line.
He showed few interests beyond foam rubber
(a new product then) and selling cars.
The only sport he played was ping pong.
As Jim Wright said much later, Frank was
an accident that kept on happening.

From the choir loft at St. John's I sang
Cesar Franck's *Panis Angelicus*
for Audrey, my nineteen-year-old sister,
elegant as Dresden porcelain
in her bridal gown. Frank in his tux
looked like he belonged on top of a cake.
Our younger sister Ginny was awestruck.

Frank sold cars at a dealership; they lived
with his folks while two sons were born.
He chased gals and the American Dream
to the Coast. Audrey wanted her own place,
but in-laws said, "Stay!" She asked for our help.
Driving a rented trailer, Dad and I sang,
"Let's answer piracy with a little burglary."

4

Carrying out cribs, we woke the in-laws.
Missus tried to bean Dad with a lampstand,
but I full-nelsoned her arms upright.
Police arrested us two trespassers,
and all us fools waited for a trial
that was dismissed. Audrey and the kids
broke camp, and she set up their new apartment.

I stayed with them a while, amusing toddlers
with campfire songs and Haydn LPs.
Both of the boys liked bouncing on my knee
to the rhythm of "Ragtime Cowboy Joe."
When the spouses reconciled, I left.
After two more sons, Frank disappeared,
but his parents co-signed for Audrey's house.

Audrey raised four boys and trolled bars
for a mate. She was a superb dancer.
Her next husband, a foreman who landscaped
the State's tollways, was steady as a stoplight
blinking by the hour at television.
He bossed the boys around; they waited on him.
A daughter was born, then prosperity.

5

I left Chicago to spin my wheels
in distant cities. On holidays,
we'd gather at Ginny's—she and her spouse,
mine, Audrey's, our kids, and Ma singing at
the piano Audrey played. When my daughter
took up the instrument, her biggest fans—
Ma and Audrey—made her feel special.

Being beautiful and kind, Audrey lived
through wars at home: her husband beat her,
the first three sons had trouble with theft,
recreational drugs, and wildly bad
marriages. One drank himself to death,
asking her for money till the end.
Another drove long-haul rigs, and found God.

Her fourth son kept to himself, craved order,
failed freshman year, but learned to make shelving;
he earned big bucks outfitting warehouses.
Her daughter, a cheerleader and "A" student,
excelled in journalism and PR.
These two scored runs for Audrey in late innings
and looked after her well until the end.

6

Audrey knew how to stay in there pitching.
A natural at her job, she tended
phones for her suburb's police department.
She would coax abused wives and suicidal
teens away from permanent solutions
to temporary problems. She knew more
about caring than many social workers.

She aided Ma through her final years.
When her second husband left, she retrieved
survivor's benefits from the first,
who through the years hadn't sent her a dime.
She and I visited more frequently.
Among friends, with her at the piano,
we sang golden oldies and drank red wine.

A pod of surviving blood relatives
assembled on her last birthday. She smiled
through the anthem and blew out candles,
declaring: "I want my health back."
Cancer and an aneurism claimed her.
Her last words to me were "You'll look younger
if you get your hair cut more often."

Journey to the Hairdresser

Sometimes I take my wife's dear mother
to the hairdresser for her weekly
freshener. She's ninety-five years old—
comfortable here with several peers
getting their color foils taken down,
washes, haircuts, twists onto curlers,
or that oxymoron "the permanent."
Heads under hairdryers, magazines
in hand, they speak their News of the World.

Arthritis has forced her to give up
making and repairing jewelry.
She gave away closets full of clothes,
forsook high-heeled shoes by the bagful.
She still tries to write checks to hungry
charities. Beautiful hair—the last-
ditch battle against disintegration.
Each time we leave I say how fine her hair looks,
and she chirps: "Rose always does a good job."

Marian

My wife's late mother collected
blue bottles excavated from eighteenth-
century middens. Designed to hold
liqueurs or medicines, their emptiness
shone cobalt in sunlit windows.

Now they carry the Christmas-morning
smile she wore as she would glide
downstairs in a full-length silk
Qing Dynasty gown brocaded
scintillating gold and blue.

Song

after Jacques Prévert

We're like a song heard on the water,
you who love me as I love you.
We'll live our life, we two together
you who love me, I who love you.

But life separates all those who love
ever so gently with little noise,
and the waves wash away every footprint
of lovers who finally must part.

Travels

DeSoto 1950

Mint green, strong as a tank, rolled
over without crumple or dent.
Bumped out a stripped fender—solid gold.
Drove till I sold it to pay the rent.

Laity and Clergy

Americans in Paris do without
peanut butter, where none is to be had;
seminaries, like cornfields during a drought,
grow fantasies enough to drive men mad.

At the Shore in Quintana Roo

A frigate bird and I curiously watch
the couple dangling from a parasail,
expanding cumulus above the sea,
a faint half-moon, and wind that will not fail.

Branding

The dollar's epigram, IN GOD WE TRUST,
won't explain how Congress members funk-shun;
lobbyists believe that that old saw must
make way for their TAKE THE MONEY, AND **RUN**.

Envoi

When you're away I miss kissing your lips,
hearing your cavils at my doing wrong,
your rosebud nipples at my fingertips,
your slippery clitoris against my tongue.

Letter to a Young Friend

Dear Tom Katt,

No man comes to harm from chasing women;
it's when we catch them the trouble starts.
My twenties were ridiculously painful—
worrying about women I might marry,
spending time with equally worried girls.
Afraid to trust. Sex sparse, usually bad,
believing even when it's bad, it's good.
Several girls I loved threw me over.

I married, had three kids, and for nine years
ate thistles in a matrimonial desert
without knowing who I was or what I wanted.
I thought one wife should be my angel,
mistress, and mother. Surely, I confused her.
We divorced and became fiery foes.

After those lean years came seven fat ones.
Available women popped up everywhere.
The group called Parents without Partners
was for me parents without principles.
The nineteen seventies—a golden age
of sexual liberation: women used
"the Pill" with no fear that it could cause cancer,
and the AIDs virus hadn't yet appeared.

How easy sowing wild oats must be
for men who don't have to pay child support.
I had a full-time job and moonlighted
with extra work to keep paying my bills.
An affair is the poor man's vacation,
and gold diggers won't set their sights on *him.*

Serial monogamy seems preferable
to promiscuity. I like knowing
intimately the one I love—without
static from some other person's karma.
Players treat lovers as commodities.

What do men look for? great legs? big boobs?
Why not health, brains, dependability,
the capacity to return affection?
Find these and the Holy Grail search is over.

What does a woman want most from a lover?
To be cared about. Selfish guys are poison.
A bunch of roses may go further
to win her heart than precious jewels would.
Some droll wag told me tired philanderers
make superb husbands. You *will* get tired.

A friend said to aged Pablo Picasso,
"You had a reputation as a ladies'
man. How do things go for you nowadays?"
"I still look," the painter said. "When I see
a beautiful woman, I ask myself,
'What would I do with a woman like that?'
I answer by just going on my way."

At days' end, a man has only three friends
in this world . . . only three . . . in this world:
an old dog, an old wife, and ready money.
Of course the world owes us a living,
but we have to work like hell to collect.

                    Yours very truly,
                    Sam Quill

Odelet to a Toad

Not much bigger than a golf ball, you
relax as stolidly as pebbled concrete.
While day lilies thrust tall and fiddlehead
ferns unfold, you wait to ambush insects.
If a passing fly eludes your tongue,
you'll find something juicy underleaf.

Can you fathom why some call you ugly?
I know you keep your warts to yourself
and can't inflict them on us humans.
Unlike athletic frogs, you stumble
when you hop. Your mien is contemplative.
You savor the places where you spend time.

Hey, I could do with more of that myself.
For you, *being* there is more important
than *getting* there. If I were to reach
down and clutch your soft body so we
might discuss this matter face to face,
I suspect that you would wet my hand.

Season Finale—the White Anemones

All summer the Perennial Revue
of flowers energized by years of composting
and crowded elbow to elbow in the front yard
have upstaged one another for sun space.
Each chorus of lungwort, bluebells, tulips,
lilies, and black-eyed Susans charmed us
for short spans of days or weeks, then bowed out
before the next bevy of ingénues.

Now October inches toward a hard frost.
Trees hold half their leaves. Some are still green.
I've raked away straggly brown chads hanging
from day lilies and bald rhizomes of iris.
Hostas, cut to the ground, show hollow stems
like stumps of graying, close-packed teeth.
Spiky rudbeckia seeds stand ready
to feed roving finches, come wintertime.

Today, white anemones steal the show
from a die-hard rose here or pale sedum there.
With petals bright as a Shasta daisy's
attached to intense green and yellow heads,
their supple necks bend in a chilly breeze.
These svelte fractals sport double and single
blossoms waving from the same plant.
Arrayed together so over-the-top

above their wilting neighbors, they will be
the last ones standing when the show closes.
Holding court with red winterberries
and blushing sweet spire, their splendor
gives pause to school kids and an elderly woman
who walk by open-mouthed. We're here for
the swan song of summer. Enjoy the day
as anemones are enjoying theirs.

About the Author

Edward Morin was born and raised in Chicago, spending summers in the Upper Peninsula of Michigan. He has a BA in philosophy from Maryknoll College (Illinois) and graduate degrees—both in English—from The University of Chicago and Loyola University.

His previous collections of poems are *The Dust of Our City* (1978), *Labor Day at Walden Pond* (1997), and a chapbook, *Housing for Wrens* (2016). *Transportation: Hot Tunes and Blues from Motor City* (1988) is a cassette recording of his original songs. He has won prizes in ten national poetry contests, and his poems have appeared in *Hudson Review, Prairie Schooner, River Styx, Poetry Northwest,* and many other magazines.

He is editor and co-translator of an anthology, *The Red Azalea: Chinese Poetry since the Cultural Revolution* (University of Hawaii Press). His co-translations of Chinese, Arabic, and Greek poetry have been published in *Iowa Review, New Letters, Banipal: Magazine of Modern Arab Literature,* and elsewhere.

His articles and reviews have appeared in *Chicago Review, Georgia Review, Michigan Quarterly Review,* and *The Detroit News.* His article, "Nature Mysticism in 'The Rose,'" is forthcoming in *A Field Guide to the Poetry of Theodore Roethke* (Ohio University Press).

The author has taught English at the Universities of Kentucky, Cincinnati, and Michigan, and at Wayne State University and College for Creative Studies. He has worked as a writer for a few large corporations and has been an editor with *Chicago Review,* Michigan State University Press, and *Peninsula Poets.*

He has acted and sung with several regional theatre and opera companies and has sung in cafes. Currently, he co-hosts a writers' workshop and public readings for The Crazy Wisdom Poetry Series in Ann Arbor, Michigan, where he and his wife live.

Kelsay Books